Europe in 12 lessons

by Pascal Fontaine

Contents

Why the European Union?

The EU's mission in the 21st century is to:

▶ maintain and build on the peace established between its member states;

▶ bring European countries together in practical cooperation;

▶ ensure that European citizens can live in security;

▶ promote economic and social solidarity;

▶ preserve European identity and diversity in a globalised world;

▶ promulgate the values that Europeans share.

I. PEACE

Before becoming a real political objective, the idea of uniting Europe was just a dream in the minds of philosophers and visionaries. Victor Hugo, for example, imagined a peaceful 'United States of Europe' inspired by humanistic ideals. The dream was shattered by the terrible wars that ravaged the continent during the first half of the 20th century.

However, a new kind of hope emerged from the rubble of the Second World War. People who had resisted totalitarianism during the war were determined to put an end to international hatred and rivalry in Europe and create the conditions for lasting peace. Between 1945 and 1950, a handful of courageous statesmen including Robert Schuman, Konrad Adenauer, Alcide de Gasperi and Winston Churchill set about persuading their peoples to enter a new era. New structures would be created in western Europe, based on shared interests and founded upon treaties guaranteeing the rule of law and equality between all countries.

Robert Schuman (French Foreign Minister) took up an idea originally conceived by Jean Monnet and, on 9 May 1950, proposed establishing a European Coal and Steel Community (ECSC). In countries which had once fought each other, the production of coal and steel would be pooled under a common High Authority. In a practical but also richly symbolic way, the raw materials of war were being turned into instruments of reconciliation and peace.

II. BRINGING EUROPE TOGETHER

The European Union encouraged German unification after the fall of the Berlin Wall in 1989. When the Soviet empire crumbled in 1991, the countries of central and eastern Europe, which had for decades endured life behind the 'iron curtain', were once again free to choose their own destiny. Many decided that their future lay within the family of democratic European nations. Eight of them joined the EU in 2004, and two more followed in 2007.

The process of EU enlargement is still going on. Entry negotiations began with Turkey and Croatia in 2005. Iceland applied in 2009 and several countries in the Balkans have set out along the road that could one day lead to EU membership. Croatia is expected to become the 28th member state of the European Union.

The fall of the Berlin Wall in 1989 led to a gradual breaking down of old divisions across the continent of Europe.

III. SECURITY

Europe in the 21st century still faces security issues. The EU has to take effective action to ensure the security of its member states. It has to work constructively with the regions just beyond its borders: the Balkans, North Africa, the Caucasus and the Middle East. It must also protect its military and strategic interests by working with its allies, especially within NATO, and by developing a genuine common European security and defence policy.

Internal and external security are two sides of the same coin. The fight against terrorism and organised crime requires the police forces of all EU countries to work together closely. Making the EU an 'area of freedom, security and justice' where everyone has equal access to justice and is equally protected by the law is a new challenge that requires close cooperation between governments. Bodies like Europol, the European Police Office and Eurojust (which promotes cooperation between prosecutors, judges and police officers in different EU countries) also have to play an active and effective role.

IV. ECONOMIC AND SOCIAL SOLIDARITY

The European Union was created to achieve political goals, and it set about achieving them through economic cooperation.

European countries account for an ever smaller percentage of the world's population. They must therefore continue pulling together if they are to ensure economic growth and be able to compete on the world stage with other major economies. No individual EU country is strong enough to go it alone in world trade. To achieve economies of scale and find new customers, European companies need a broader base than just their national home market, and the European single market provides it. To ensure that as many people as possible benefit from this Europe-wide market of 500 million consumers, the EU is endeavouring to remove obstacles to trade and is working to free businesses from unnecessary red tape.

But Europe-wide free competition must be counterbalanced by Europe-wide solidarity. This has clear tangible benefits for European citizens: when they fall victim to floods and other natural disasters, they receive assistance from the EU budget. The 'Structural Funds', managed by the European Commission, encourage and supplement the efforts of the EU's national and regional authorities to reduce inequalities between different parts of Europe. Money from the EU budget and loans from the European Investment Bank (EIB) are used to improve Europe's transport infrastructure (for example, to extend the network of motorways and high-speed railways), thus providing better access to outlying regions and boosting trans-European trade.

The global financial crisis in 2008 triggered the sharpest economic downturn in the EU's history. Governments and EU institutions had to act swiftly to rescue banks, and the EU provided financial assistance to the hardest-hit countries. Sharing a single currency helped protect the euro area against speculation and devaluation. Then, in 2010, the EU and its member states made a concerted effort to reduce their public debt. The big challenge for European countries in the years ahead will be to stand together in the face of global crises and to find, together, a way out of recession and into sustainable growth.

V. EUROPEAN IDENTITY AND DIVERSITY IN A GLOBALISED WORLD

Europe's post-industrial societies are becoming increasingly complex. Standards of living have risen steadily, but there are still significant gaps between rich and poor. These gaps may be widened by factors such as economic recession, industrial relocation, the ageing of the population and problems with public finances. It is important for EU countries to work together to tackle these problems.

But working together does not mean erasing the distinct cultural and linguistic identity of individual countries. On the contrary, many EU activities help promote regional specialities and the rich diversity of Europe's traditions and cultures.

In the long run, all EU countries benefit. Sixty years of European integration has shown that the EU as a whole is greater than the sum of its parts. It has much more economic, social, technological, commercial and political clout than if its member states had to act individually. There is added value in acting together and speaking with a single voice.

United in diversity: working together achieves better results.

In today's world, rising economies such as China, India and Brazil are set to join the United States as global superpowers. It is therefore more vital than ever for the member states of the European Union to come together and achieve a 'critical mass', thus maintaining their influence on the world stage.

How does the EU exercise this influence?

▶ The European Union is the world's leading trading power and therefore plays a decisive role in international negotiations, such as those among the 153 member countries of the World Trade Organisation (WTO), or at the United Nations conferences on climate change.

▶ The EU takes a clear position on sensitive issues affecting ordinary people, such as environmental protection, renewable energy resources, the 'precautionary principle' in food safety, the ethical aspects of biotechnology, the need to protect endangered species, etc.

▶ The EU remains at the forefront of global efforts to tackle global warming. In December 2008 it unilaterally committed itself to a 20 % cut in greenhouse gas emissions by 2020.

The old saying 'unity is strength' is thus as relevant as ever to today's Europeans.

VI. VALUES

The EU wishes to promote humanitarian and progressive values, and ensure that humankind is the beneficiary, rather than the victim, of the great global changes that are taking place. People's needs cannot be met simply by market forces, or by individual countries taking unilateral action.

So the EU stands for a view of humanity and a model of society that the great majority of its citizens support. Europeans cherish their rich heritage of values, which includes a belief in human rights, social solidarity, free enterprise, a fair distribution of the fruits of economic growth, the right to a protected environment, respect for cultural, linguistic and religious diversity and a harmonious blend of tradition and progress.

The Charter of Fundamental Rights of the European Union was proclaimed in Nice in December 2000. It is now legally binding thanks to the Treaty of Lisbon, which came into force on 1 December 2009. The Charter sets out all the rights recognised today by the EU's member states and their citizens. Shared rights and values create a feeling of kinship between Europeans. To take just one example, all EU countries have abolished the death penalty.

[2]

▶ 1951: The European Coal and Steel Community is set up by the six founding members.

▶ 1957: The same six countries sign the Treaties of Rome, setting up the European Economic Community (EEC) and the European Atomic Energy Community (Euratom).

▶ 1973: The Communities expand to nine member states and introduce more common policies.

▶ 1979: The first direct elections to the European Parliament.

▶ 1981: The first Mediterranean enlargement.

▶ 1992: The European single market becomes a reality.

▶ 1993: The Treaty of Maastricht establishes the European Union (EU).

▶ 2002: The euro comes into circulation.

▶ 2007: The EU has 27 member states.

▶ 2009: The Lisbon Treaty comes into force, changing the way the EU works.

1.

On 9 May 1950, the Schuman Declaration proposed the establishment of a European Coal and Steel Community, which became reality with the Treaty of Paris of 18 April 1951. This put in place a common market in coal and steel between the six founding countries (Belgium, the Federal Republic of Germany, France, Italy, Luxembourg and the Netherlands). The aim, in the aftermath of the Second World War, was to secure peace between Europe's victorious and vanquished nations and bring them together as equals, cooperating within shared institutions.

2.

The 'Six' then decided, with the Treaties of Rome on 25 March 1957, to set up a European Atomic Energy Community (Euratom) and a European Economic Community (EEC). The latter would involve building a wider common market covering a whole range of goods and services. Customs duties between the six countries were abolished on 1 July 1968 and common policies, notably on trade and agriculture, were also put in place during the 1960s.

3.

So successful was this venture that Denmark, Ireland and the United Kingdom decided to join. This first enlargement, from six to nine members, took place in 1973. At the same time, new social and environmental policies were introduced, and the European Regional Development Fund (ERDF) was set up in 1975.

On 9 May 1950, French Foreign Minister Robert Schuman first publicly proposed the ideas that led to the European Union. So 9 May is celebrated as the EU's birthday.

4.

June 1979 saw a decisive step forward, with the first elections to the European Parliament by direct universal suffrage. These elections are held every five years.

5.

In 1981, Greece joined the Communities, followed by Spain and Portugal in 1986. This expansion of the Communities into southern Europe made it all the more necessary to implement regional aid programmes.

6.

The worldwide economic recession in the early 1980s brought with it a wave of 'euro-pessimism'. However, hope sprang anew in 1985 when the European Commission, under its President Jacques Delors, published a White Paper setting out a timetable for completing the European single market by 1 January 1993. This ambitious goal was enshrined in the Single European Act, which was signed in February 1986 and came into force on 1 July 1987.

7.

The political shape of Europe was dramatically changed when the Berlin Wall fell in 1989. This led to the unification of Germany in October 1990 and the coming of democracy to the countries of central and eastern Europe as they broke away from Soviet control. The Soviet Union itself ceased to exist in December 1991.

At the same time, the EEC member states were negotiating a new treaty, which was adopted by the European Council (the meeting of presidents and/or prime ministers) at Maastricht in December 1991. By adding intergovernmental cooperation (in areas such as foreign policy and internal security) to the existing Community system, the Maastricht Treaty created the European Union (EU). It came into force on 1 November 1993.

8.

Three more countries – Austria, Finland and Sweden – joined the European Union in 1995, bringing its membership to 15. By then, Europe was facing the growing challenges of globalisation. New technologies and the ever-increasing use of the Internet were modernising economies but also creating social and cultural tensions. At the same time, unemployment and the rising cost of pensions were putting pressure on national economies, making reform all the more necessary. Voters were increasingly calling on their governments to find practical solutions to these problems.

In March 2000, therefore, EU leaders adopted the 'Lisbon strategy'. It was designed to enable the European Union to compete on the world market with other major players such as the United States and the newly industrialised countries. The aim was to encourage innovation and business investment, and to ensure that Europe's education systems met the needs of the information society.

Meanwhile, the EU was working on its most spectacular project to date — creating a single currency to make life easier for businesses, consumers and travellers. On 1 January 2002, the euro replaced the old currencies of 12 EU countries, which together made up the 'euro area'. The euro is now a major world currency alongside the US dollar.

9.

In the mid-1990s, preparations began for the biggest-ever EU enlargement. Membership applications were received from the six former Soviet-bloc countries (Bulgaria, the Czech Republic, Hungary, Poland, Romania and Slovakia), the three Baltic states that had been part of the Soviet Union (Estonia, Latvia and Lithuania), one of the republics of former Yugoslavia (Slovenia) and two Mediterranean countries (Cyprus and Malta).

The EU welcomed this chance to help stabilise the European continent and to extend the benefits of European integration to the young democracies. Negotiations opened in December 1997 and 10 of the candidate countries joined the European Union on 1 May 2004. Bulgaria and Romania followed on 1 January 2007, bringing the EU's membership to 27.

10.

To enable it to face the complex challenges of the 21st century, the enlarged EU needed a simpler and more efficient method for taking its joint decisions. New rules had been proposed in a draft EU Constitution, signed in October 2004, which would have replaced all the existing treaties. But this text was rejected by two national referendums in 2005. The Constitution was therefore replaced by the Treaty of Lisbon, which was signed on 13 December 2007 and came into force on 1 December 2009. It amends but does not replace the previous treaties, and it introduces most of the changes that featured in the Constitution. For example, it gives the European Council a permanent President and creates the post of High Representative of the Union for Foreign Affairs and Security Policy.

Enlarging the EU and getting on with the neighbours

▶ The European Union is open to any European country that fulfils the democratic, political and economic criteria for membership.

▶ Successive enlargements (the most recent being in 2007) have increased the EU's membership from six to 27 countries. As of 2010, nine other countries are either negotiating membership (e.g. Croatia and Turkey) or are in different stages of preparation. Croatia is set to become the 28th member state of the European Union.

▶ Each treaty admitting a new member requires the unanimous approval of all member states. In addition, in advance of each new enlargement, the EU must assess its capacity to absorb the new member(s) and the ability of its institutions to continue to function properly.

▶ Enlarging the European Union has helped strengthen and stabilise democracy and security in Europe and increase the continent's potential for trade and economic growth.

I. UNITING A CONTINENT

(a) A union of 27

When it met in Copenhagen in December 2002, the European Council took one of the most momentous steps in the history of European integration. By inviting 12 more countries to join it, the European Union was not simply increasing its geographical size and population; it was putting an end to the division which had split our continent in two since 1945. European countries which, for decades, had not enjoyed democratic freedom were finally able to rejoin the family of democratic European nations. Thus the Czech Republic, Estonia, Hungary, Latvia, Lithuania, Poland, Slovakia and Slovenia became EU members in 2004, together with the Mediterranean islands of Cyprus and Malta. Bulgaria and Romania followed in 2007. All are now partners in the momentous project conceived by the EU's founding fathers.

(b) Negotiations under way

Turkey, a member of NATO with a long-standing association agreement with the EU, applied for European Union membership in 1987. Given Turkey's geographical location and political history, the EU hesitated for a long time before accepting its application. However, in October 2005, accession negotiations finally began — not only with Turkey but also with Croatia. As of 2010, the negotiations with Croatia were near completion. Some EU countries have expressed doubts as to whether Turkey will or should become a member of the European Union. They propose an alternative arrangement — a 'privileged partnership' — but Turkey rejects this idea.

(c) The western Balkans and Iceland

The western Balkan countries, most of which were once part of Yugoslavia, are also turning to the European Union to speed up their economic reconstruction, improve their mutual relations (long scarred by ethnic and religious wars) and consolidate their democratic institutions. In 2005, the EU gave 'candidate country' status to the former Yugoslav Republic of Macedonia. Potential candidates are Albania, Bosnia and Herzegovina, Montenegro and Serbia, each of which has a 'stabilisation and association' agreement with the EU, designed to pave the way for eventual membership talks. Iceland, hard hit by the financial crisis in 2008, applied for EU membership in 2009. Kosovo declared its independence on 18 February 2008 and could also become an official candidate country.

By the end of this decade, therefore, European Union membership could grow from 27 to 35 countries. This would be another major enlargement and would probably require further changes in the way the EU works.

II. MEMBERSHIP CONDITIONS

(a) Legal requirements

European integration has always been a political and economic process, open to all European countries that are prepared to sign up to the Treaties and take on board the full body of EU law. According to the Lisbon Treaty (Article 49), any European state may apply to become a member of the European Union provided it respects the principles of liberty, democracy, respect for human rights and fundamental freedoms, and the rule of law.

(b) The 'Copenhagen criteria'

In 1993, following requests from the former communist countries to join the Union, the European Council laid down three criteria they should fulfil so as to become members. By the time they join, new members must have:

▸ stable institutions guaranteeing democracy, the rule of law, human rights and respect for and protection of minorities;

▸ a functioning market economy and the capacity to cope with competitive pressure and market forces within the Union;

▸ the ability to take on the obligations of membership, including support for the aims of the Union. They must have a public administration capable of applying and managing EU laws in practice.

The 'Pearl of the Adriatic' — Dubrovnik in Croatia, a candidate for EU membership.

(c) The process of becoming an EU member state

Membership talks ('accession negotiations') take place between the candidate country and the European Commission, which represents the EU. Once these are concluded, the decision to allow this country to join the EU must be taken unanimously by the existing member states meeting in the Council. The European Parliament must also give its assent, which means an absolute majority of its members must vote in favour. The accession treaty must then be ratified by the member states and the candidate country, each in accordance with its own constitutional procedure.

During the negotiation period, candidate countries normally receive EU 'accession partnership' aid to help them catch up economically. They also usually have 'stabilisation and association agreements' with the EU. Under these agreements, the EU directly monitors the economic and administrative reforms the candidate countries have to carry out in order to meet the conditions for EU membership.

III. HOW LARGE CAN THE EU BECOME?

(a) Geographical frontiers

In most EU countries, discussions about the proposed Constitutional Treaty showed that many Europeans are concerned about where the borders of the European Union should be drawn, and even about Europe's identity. There are no simple answers to these questions, particularly since each country views its geopolitical or economic interests differently. The Baltic countries and Poland are in favour of Ukraine joining the EU, so what about Ukraine's neighbours? Difficulties arise from the political situation in Belarus and the strategic position of Moldova. If Turkey joins the EU, then what about Armenia, Georgia and other countries in the Caucasus?

The EU gives financal aid to help build the economy in neighbouring countries.

Despite fulfilling the conditions, Liechtenstein, Norway and Switzerland are not members of the European Union because public opinion in those countries is currently against joining.

In different EU countries, public opinion is more or less divided over the question of the European Union's final frontiers. If geographical criteria alone were applied, taking no account of democratic values, the EU could — like the Council of Europe (not an EU body) — end up with 47 member states including Russia. But Russian membership would clearly create unacceptable imbalances in the European Union, both politically and geographically.

The sensible approach is to say that any European country is entitled to apply for EU membership provided it can take on board the full body of EU law and is prepared to adopt the euro. European integration has been a continuous process since 1950, and any attempt to fix the EU's boundaries once and for all would run counter to that process.

(b) Neighbourhood policy

Enlargements in 2004 and 2007 pushed the European Union's borders further east and south, raising the question of how the EU should handle relations with its new neighbours. Stability and security are an issue in the regions beyond its borders, and the European Union wished to avoid the emergence of new dividing lines between itself and these neighbouring regions. For example, action was needed to tackle emerging threats to security such as illegal immigration, the disruption of energy supplies, environmental degradation, organised cross-border crime and terrorism. So the EU developed a new European neighbourhood policy (ENP), governing relations with its neighbours to the east (Armenia, Azerbaijan, Belarus, Georgia, Moldova and Ukraine), and to the south (Algeria, Egypt, Israel, Jordan, Lebanon, Libya, Morocco, the occupied Palestinian territory, Syria and Tunisia).

Almost all these countries have bilateral 'partnership and cooperation' agreements or association agreements with the EU, under which they are committed to common values (such as democracy, human rights and the rule of law) and to making progress towards a market economy, sustainable development and reducing poverty. The EU, for its part, offers financial, technical and macroeconomic assistance, easier access to visas and a range of measures to help these countries develop.

Since 1995, the southern Mediterranean countries have been linked to the European Union through political, economic and diplomatic ties known as the 'Barcelona process', later re-named the Euro-Mediterranean Partnership. At a summit meeting in Paris in July 2008, this partnership was relaunched as the Union for the Mediterranean, bringing together the 27 member states of the European Union and 16 partner countries across the southern Mediterranean and the Middle East.

The EU's financial assistance to both groups of countries is managed by the European Neighbourhood and Partnership Instrument (ENPI). Its overall budget for 2007-13 is approximately € 12 billion.

▶ The EU's Heads of State and/or Government meet, as the European Council, to set the EU's overall political direction and to take major decisions on key issues.

▶ The Council, made up of ministers from the EU member states, meets frequently to take policy decisions and make EU laws.

▶ The European Parliament, which represents the people, shares legislative and budgetary power with the Council.

▶ The European Commission, which represents the common interest of the EU, is the main executive body. It puts forward proposals for legislation and ensures that EU policies are properly implemented.

I. THE DECISION-MAKING INSTITUTIONS

The European Union is more than just a confederation of countries, but it is not a federal state. In fact, its structure does not fall into any traditional legal category. It is historically unique, and its decision-making system has been constantly evolving for the past 60 years or so.

The Treaties (known as 'primary' legislation) are the basis for a large body of 'secondary' legislation which has a direct impact on the daily lives of EU citizens. The secondary legislation consists mainly of regulations, directives and recommendations adopted by the EU institutions.

These laws, along with EU policies in general, are the result of decisions taken by the Council (representing national governments), the European Parliament (representing the people) and the European Commission (a body independent of EU governments that upholds the collective European interest). Other institutions and bodies also play a role, as outlined below.

(a) The European Council

The European Council is the EU's top political institution. It consists of the Heads of State or Government — the presidents and/or prime ministers — of all the EU member countries, plus the President of the European Commission (see below). It normally meets four times a year, in Brussels. It has a permanent President, whose job is to coordinate the European Council's work and ensure its continuity. The permanent President is elected (by a qualified majority vote of its members) for a period of two and a half years and can be re-elected once. The former Belgian Prime Minister, Herman Van Rompuy, has occupied this post since 1 December 2009.

The European Council fixes the EU's goals and sets the course for achieving them. It provides the impetus for the EU's main policy initiatives and takes decisions on thorny issues that the Council of Ministers has not been able to agree on. The European Council also tackles current international problems via the 'common foreign and security policy' — which is a mechanism for coordinating the foreign policies of the EU's member states.

(b) The Council

The Council (also known as the Council of Ministers) is made up of ministers from the EU's national governments. The member states take it in turns to hold the Council Presidency for a six-month period. Every Council meeting is attended by one minister from each EU country. Which ministers attend a meeting depends on which topic is on the agenda: foreign affairs, agriculture, industry, transport, the environment, etc.

The Council's main job is to pass EU laws. Normally it shares this responsibility with the European Parliament. The Council and the Parliament also share equal responsibility for adopting the EU budget. In addition, the Council signs international agreements that have been negotiated by the Commission.

According to the Lisbon Treaty, the Council has to take its decisions either by a simple majority vote, a 'qualified majority' vote or unanimously, depending on the subject to be decided.

The Council has to agree unanimously on important questions such as taxation, amending the Treaties, launching a new common policy or allowing a new country to join the Union.

In most other cases, qualified majority voting is used. This means that a Council decision is adopted if a specified minimum number of votes are cast in its favour. The number of votes allocated to each EU country roughly reflects the size of its population.

Until 1 November 2014, assuming the EU still has 27 member states, a decision is adopted if:

▶ at least 255 of the 347 votes (i.e. 73.91 %) are cast in favour;

▶ it is approved by a majority of member states, i.e. at least 14;

▶ if these favourable member states represent at least 62 % of the EU's population.

A more democratic Europe: thanks to the Lisbon Treaty, European citizens can now propose new laws.

From 1 November 2014, according to the Lisbon Treaty, the system will be simplified. A decision will be adopted if 55 % of the member states (i.e. at least 15 of them) are in favour of it and if they represent at least 65 % of the EU's population.

(c) The European Parliament (EP)

The European Parliament is the elected body that represents the EU's citizens. It supervises the EU's activities and, together with the Council, it enacts EU legislation. Since 1979, members of the European Parliament (MEPs) have been directly elected, by universal suffrage, every five years

After the last EP elections, in June 2009, the former Polish Prime Minister Jerzy Buzek (European People's Party) was elected President of the Parliament for a period of two and a half years.

The European Parliament — this is where you can make your voice heard.

Parliament holds its major debates at monthly gatherings (known as 'plenary sessions') attended, in principle, by all MEPs. These plenary sessions are normally held in Strasbourg, and any additional sessions are held in Brussels. The preparatory work is also usually done in Brussels: the 'Conference of Presidents' — i.e. the chairmen of the political groups together with the President of Parliament — sets the agenda for the plenary sessions while 20 parliamentary committees draft the legislative amendments that are to be debated. Parliament's day-to-day administrative work is done by its General Secretariat, based in Luxembourg and Brussels. Each political group also has its own secretariat.

Number of seats in the European Parliament per country following the elections in 2009

Austria	17	Latvia	8
Belgium	22	Lithuania	12
Bulgaria	17	Luxembourg	6
Cyprus	6	Malta	5
Czech Republic	22	Netherlands	25
Denmark	13	Poland	50
Estonia	6	Portugal	22
Finland	13	Romania	33
France	72	Slovakia	13
Germany	99	Slovenia	7
Greece	22	Spain	50
Hungary	22	Sweden	18
Ireland	12	United Kingdom	72
Italy	72		
TOTAL			**736**

NB: A decision according to Protocol No 36 to the Treaty of Lisbon will temporarily increase the total number of MEPs to 754, until the next elections in 2014.

The Parliament takes part in the legislative work of the EU in two ways.

▸ Via **'co-decision'**, which is the **ordinary legislative procedure**, Parliament shares equal responsibility with the Council for legislating in all policy areas that require a 'qualified majority' vote in the Council. Since the Lisbon Treaty came into force, these areas cover about 95 % of EU legislation. Council and Parliament can reach an agreement as soon as the first reading. If they cannot agree after two readings, the proposal is brought before a conciliation committee.

▸ Via the **'assent'** procedure, Parliament must ratify the EU's international agreements (negotiated by the Commission), including any new treaty enlarging the European Union.

The political groups in the European Parliament

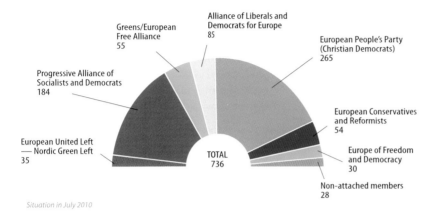

Greens/European Free Alliance
55

Alliance of Liberals and Democrats for Europe
85

European People's Party (Christian Democrats)
265

Progressive Alliance of Socialists and Democrats
184

European People's Party (Christian Democrats)
265

European Conservatives and Reformists
54

European United Left — Nordic Green Left
35

TOTAL
736

Europe of Freedom and Democracy
30

Non-attached members
28

Situation in July 2010

The European Parliament also shares with the Council equal responsibility for adopting the EU budget (proposed by the European Commission). The Parliament can reject the proposed budget, and it has already done so on several occasions. When this happens, the entire budget procedure has to be restarted. By using its budgetary powers Parliament exercises considerable influence over EU policymaking.

Last but not least, the European Parliament exercises democratic supervision over the Union, and in particular over the European Commission. Every five years, when the time comes to appoint a new Commission, the newly elected European Parliament can – by a simple majority vote – approve or reject the European Council's nominee for the post of Commission President. Clearly, this vote will reflect the results of the recent EP elections. Parliament also interviews each proposed member of the Commission before voting on whether to approve the new Commission as a whole.

At any time, Parliament can dismiss the whole Commission by adopting a motion of censure. This requires a two thirds majority. Parliament also supervises the day-to-day management of EU policies by putting oral and written questions to the Commission and the Council.

(d) The European Commission

The Commission is a key EU institution. It alone has the right to draw up proposals for new EU legislation, which it sends to the Council and Parliament for discussion and adoption.

Its members are appointed for a five-year term by agreement between the member states, subject to approval by the European Parliament (as described above). The Commission is answerable to the Parliament, and the entire Commission has to resign if the Parliament passes a motion of censure against it.

There is one Commission member ('Commissioner') from each EU country, including the Commission President and the High Representative of the Union for Foreign Affairs and Security Policy, who is one of the Commission's vice-presidents.

On 9 February 2010, the European Parliament voted to approve the new Commission. The former Prime Minister of Portugal, José Manuel Barroso, was reappointed President of the Commission for a second five-year term.

The Commission enjoys a substantial degree of independence in exercising its powers. Its job is to uphold the common interest, which means that it must not take instructions from any national government. As 'Guardian of the Treaties', it has to ensure that the regulations and directives adopted by the Council and Parliament are being implemented in the member states. If they are not, the Commission can take the offending party to the Court of Justice to oblige it to comply with EU law.

As the EU's executive arm, the Commission implements the decisions taken by the Council in areas such as the common agricultural policy. It has wide powers to manage the EU's common policies, such as research and technology, overseas aid and regional development. It also manages the budget for these policies.

The Commissioners are assisted by a civil service, based mainly in Brussels and Luxembourg, divided into 43 departments and services. There are also a number of agencies, set up to carry out specific tasks for the Commission and mostly located in other European cities.

(e) The Court of Justice

The Court of Justice of the European Union, located in Luxembourg, is made up of one judge from each EU country, assisted by eight advocates-general. They are appointed by joint agreement of the governments of the member states for a renewable term of six years. Their independence is guaranteed. The Court's role is to ensure that EU law is complied with, and that the Treaties are correctly interpreted and applied.

(f) The European Central Bank

The European Central Bank (ECB), in Frankfurt, is responsible for managing the euro and the EU's monetary policy (see Chapter 7 'The euro'). Its main task is to maintain price stability in the euro area. The Central Bank acquired the status of EU institution under the Treaty of Lisbon.

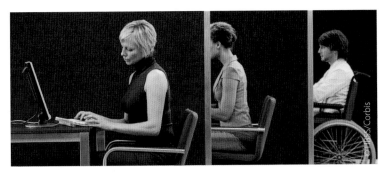

The Court of Justice ensures that European law is fully respected. It has, for example, confirmed that discrimination of handicapped workers is forbidden.

(g) The Court of Auditors

The European Court of Auditors, located in Luxembourg, was established in 1975. It has one member from each EU country, appointed for a term of six years by agreement between the member states following consultation of the European Parliament. It checks that all the European Union's revenue has been received and all its expenditure incurred in a lawful and regular manner and that the EU budget has been managed soundly.

II. OTHER BODIES

(a) The European Economic and Social Committee

When taking decisions in a number of policy areas, the Council and Commission consult the European Economic and Social Committee (EESC). Its members represent the various economic and social interest groups that collectively make up 'organised civil society', and are appointed by the Council for a five-year term.

(b) The Committee of the Regions

The Committee of the Regions (CoR) consists of representatives of regional and local government. They are proposed by the member states and appointed by the Council for a five-year term. The Council and Commission must consult the CoR on matters of relevance to the regions, and it may also issue opinions on its own initiative.

(c) The European Investment Bank

The European Investment Bank (EIB), based in Luxembourg, provides loans and guarantees to help the EU's less developed regions and to help make businesses more competitive.

[**5**]

▶ The European Union acts in a wide range of policy areas where its action is beneficial to the member states. These include:

- innovation policies, which bring state-of-the-art technologies to fields such as environmental protection, research and development (R & D) and energy;

- solidarity policies (also known as cohesion policies) in regional, agricultural and social affairs.

▶ The Union funds these policies through an annual budget which enables it to complement and add value to action taken by national governments. The EU budget is small by comparison with the collective wealth of its member states: it represents no more than 1.23 % of their combined gross national income.

I. INNOVATION POLICIES

The European Union's activities impact on the day-to-day life of its citizens by addressing the real challenges facing society: environmental protection, health, technological innovation, energy, etc.

(a) The environment and sustainable development

The EU aims to help prevent climate change by seriously reducing its greenhouse gas emissions. In December 2008, the European Council agreed that, by 2020, the European Union would cut its emissions by at least 20% (compared with 1990 levels), raise renewable energy's share of the market to 20% and cut overall energy consumption by 20%. It was also agreed that 10% of fuel for transport should come from biofuels, electricity or hydrogen.

At the Copenhagen summit on 19 December 2009, the EU tried to persuade other major powers to adopt the same goals — but it was only partially successful. All parties accepted the need to limit global warming to an average increase of 2 °C above pre-industrial levels, but as yet there is no guarantee of a collective commitment to achieving this goal. Nevertheless, the European Union did secure a deal whereby developed countries will provide € 20 billion to finance developing countries' action on climate change.

The EU is at the forefront of the fight to prevent climate change
and encourage sustainable development.

The EU is also tackling a wide range of other environmental issues including noise, waste, the protection of natural habitats, exhaust gases, chemicals, industrial accidents and the cleanliness of bathing water. It is also planning a collective approach to preventing natural or man-made disasters such as oil spills or forest fires.

The European Union is constantly improving its legislation to provide better protection for public health. For example, EU legislation on chemicals has been reworked, replacing earlier piecemeal rules with a single system known as REACH – which stands for the Registration, Evaluation and Authorisation of Chemicals. This system uses a central database, managed (since 2008) by the European Chemicals Agency, located in Helsinki. The aim is to prevent contamination of the air, water, soil and buildings, to preserve biodiversity and to improve the health and safety of EU citizens while at the same time keeping European industry competitive.

(b) Technological innovation

The founders of the European Union rightly saw that Europe's future prosperity would depend on its ability to remain a world leader in technology. They saw the advantages to be gained from joint European research. So, in 1958, alongside the EEC, they established Euratom – the European Atomic Energy Community. Its aim was for EU countries together to exploit nuclear energy for peaceful purposes, with the help of a Joint Research Centre (JRC). This consists of seven institutes at five locations: Ispra (Italy), Karlsruhe (Germany), Petten (the Netherlands), Geel (Belgium) and Seville (Spain).

However, to keep pace with increasing global competition, European research had to diversify – and to break down the barriers between national research programmes, bringing together as wide a variety of scientists as possible and helping them find industrial applications for their discoveries.

Joint research at EU level is designed to complement national research programmes. It focuses on projects that bring together a number of laboratories in several EU countries. It also supports fundamental research in fields such as controlled thermonuclear fusion – a potentially inexhaustible source of energy for the 21st century. Moreover, it encourages research and technological development in key industries such as electronics and computers, which face stiff competition from outside Europe.

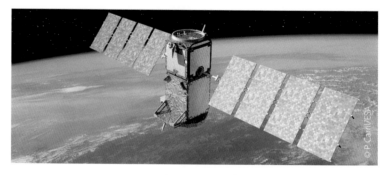

The EU encourages innovation and research such as 'Galileo', Europe's own global navigation satellite system.

The EU's goal is to spend 3 % of its GDP on research. The main vehicle for funding EU research is a series of 'framework' programmes. The seventh research and technological development framework programme covers the period 2007-13. Most of the € 50-billion-plus budget is being spent on research in areas like health, food and agriculture, information and communication technologies, nanosciences, energy, the environment, transport, security and space and socioeconomic sciences. Other programmes promote international cooperation on leading-edge research projects and provide support for researchers and their career development.

(c) Energy

Fossil fuels — oil, natural gas and coal — provide 80 % of the energy consumed in the EU. A large and growing proportion of these fossil fuels is imported from outside the EU. At present, 50 % of gas and oil is imported, and this dependence could grow to 70 % by 2030. The EU will thus be more vulnerable to cuts in supply or price hikes caused by international crises. Another reason to reduce its consumption of fossil fuels is to reverse the process of global warming.

Various steps will have to be taken in future, such as saving energy by using it more intelligently, developing alternative energy sources (particularly renewable energy sources in Europe), and increasing international cooperation. Energy R & D in Europe focuses on solar, wind, biomass and nuclear power. There are also pilot projects to develop CO_2 capture and storage and to make hydrogen fuel cell vehicles commercially viable. The EU has also invested € 1.6 billion in the 'clean sky' project for developing less polluting aircraft.

II. SOLIDARITY POLICIES

To make sure the single market (see Chapter 6) works properly, imbalances in that market need to be corrected. That is the purpose of the EU's 'solidarity policies', designed to help underdeveloped regions and troubled sectors of the economy. The EU must also play its part in helping restructure industries which have been hard hit by fast-growing international competition.

(a) Regional aid

Under the EU's regional policy, European Union funds are used to boost development in regions lagging behind, to rejuvenate industrial areas in decline, to help young people and the long-term unemployed find work, to modernise farming and to help less-favoured rural areas.

The funds earmarked for regional aid in 2007-13 are targeted at three objectives.

▶ **Convergence:** the aim here is to help the least-developed countries and regions catch up more quickly with the EU average by improving conditions for growth and employment. This is done by investing in physical and human capital, innovation, the knowledge society, adaptability, the environment and administrative efficiency.

▶ **Regional competitiveness and employment:** the objective is to increase the competitiveness, employment levels and attractiveness of regions other than the least-developed ones. The way to make this happen is to anticipate economic and social changes and to promote innovation, entrepreneurship, environmental protection, accessibility, adaptability and the development of inclusive job markets.

▶ **European territorial cooperation:** the objective here is to increase cross-border, transnational and interregional cooperation, helping neighbouring authorities find joint solutions to shared problems in sectors such as urban, rural and coastal development. For example, countries and regional authorities along the Danube river and on the Baltic sea share common strategies for sustainable development in those regions.

These objectives are financed by specific EU funds, known as the 'Structural Funds', which top up or stimulate investment by the private sector and by national and regional governments.

▶ **The European Regional Development Fund** (ERDF) is used to finance regional development projects and to boost the economy in regions that are lagging behind. This includes the redevelopment of declining industrial areas.

▶ **The European Social Fund** (ESF) is used to finance vocational training and to help people find work.

In addition to the Structural Funds, there is a Cohesion Fund, which is used to finance transport infrastructure and environmental projects in EU countries whose GDP per capita is lower than 90 % of the EU average.

(b) The common agricultural policy (CAP) and common fisheries policy (CFP)

The aims of the CAP, as set out in the original Treaty of Rome from 1957, were to ensure a fair standard of living for farmers, to stabilise markets, to ensure that supplies reach consumers at reasonable prices and to modernise farming infrastructure. These goals have largely been achieved. Moreover, consumers today enjoy security of supply and the prices of agricultural products are kept stable, protected from fluctuations on the world market. The policy is financed by the European Agricultural Guarantee Fund (EAGF) and the European Agricultural Fund for Rural Development (EAFRD).

However, the CAP became a victim of its own success. Production grew far faster than consumption, placing a heavy burden on the EU budget. In order to resolve this problem, agricultural policy had to be redefined. This reform is beginning to show results: production has been curbed.

Agriculture must provide safe food of good quality.

The new role of the farming community is to ensure a certain amount of economic activity in every rural area and to protect the diversity of Europe's countryside. This diversity and the recognition of a 'rural way of life' — people living in harmony with the land — are an important part of Europe's identity. Furthermore, European agriculture has an important role to play in combating climate change, protecting wildlife and feeding the world.

The European Commission represents the EU in international negotiations at the World Trade Organisation (WTO). The EU wants the WTO to put more emphasis on food quality, the precautionary principle ('better safe than sorry') and animal welfare.

From 2013 onwards, the European Commission wants the CAP to give priority to making European agriculture sustainable, giving farmers sufficient protection from volatile markets, preserving biodiversity and protecting local and regional speciality products.

The European Union has also begun reforming its fisheries policy. The main aim here is to preserve stocks of fish (such as the endangered bluefin tuna) and to reduce the overcapacity of fishing fleets while providing financial assistance for people who leave the fishing industry.

(c) The social dimension
The aim of the EU's social policy is to correct the most glaring inequalities in European society. The European Social Fund (ESF) was established in 1961 to promote job creation and help workers move from one type of work and/or one geographical area to another.

Financial aid is not the only way in which the EU seeks to improve social conditions in Europe. Aid alone could never solve all the problems caused by economic recession or by regional underdevelopment. The dynamic effects of growth must, above all, encourage social progress. This goes hand in hand with legislation that guarantees a solid set of minimum rights. Some of these rights are enshrined in the Treaties, e.g. the right of women and men to equal pay for equal work. Others are set out in directives concerning the protection of workers (health and safety at work) and essential safety standards.

The Charter of Basic Social Rights, which became an integral part of the Treaty in 1997, sets out the rights that all workers in the EU should enjoy: free movement; fair pay; improved working conditions; social protection; the right to form associations and to undertake collective bargaining; the right to vocational training; equal treatment of women and men; worker information, consultation and participation; health protection and safety at the workplace; protection for children, the elderly and the disabled.

III. PAYING FOR EUROPE: THE EU BUDGET

To fund its policies, the European Union has an annual budget which, in 2010, amounted to more than € 140 billion. This budget is financed by what are called the EU's 'own resources', which cannot exceed 1.23 % of the total gross national income of all the member states.

These resources are mainly drawn from:

▶ customs duties on products imported into the EU, including farm levies;

▶ a percentage of the value added tax (VAT) levied on goods and services throughout the EU;

▶ contributions from the member states, reflecting the wealth of each country.

Each annual budget is part of a seven-year budget cycle known as the 'financial perspective'. The financial perspectives are drawn up by the European Commission and require unanimous approval from the member states and negotiation and agreement with the European Parliament. The next financial perspective will be for 2013-20.

The breakdown in spending can be illustrated by the 2010 budget:

▶ competitiveness and cohesion: € 64 billion, including the Structural Funds, the Cohesion Fund, the research programmes and the trans-European transport and energy networks;

▶ managing natural resources: € 60 billion, mainly for farming and rural development;

▶ 'citizenship, freedom, security and justice' (see Chapter 10): € 1.6 billion;

▶ the EU as a global partner (aid, trade, etc.): € 8 billion;

▶ administrative expenses: € 8 billion.

WHO DOES WHAT? HOW RESPONSIBILITIES ARE SHARED BETWEEN THE EU AND ITS MEMBER STATES

The European Union alone is responsible for:

- customs union
- rules governing competition within the single market
- monetary policy for countries using the euro
- conservation of marine biological resources under the common fisheries policy
- common commercial policy
- concluding an international agreement when this is provided for in EU legislation

The European Union and its member states share responsibility for:

- the single market
- aspects of social policy as defined in the Lisbon Treaty
- economic and social cohesion
- agriculture and fisheries, except for the conservation of marine biological resources
- the environment
- consumer protection
- transport
- trans-European networks
- energy
- creating an area of freedom, security and justice
- aspects of common security challenges relating to public health, as defined in the Treaty of Lisbon
- research, technological development and space
- development cooperation and humanitarian aid

Fields for which the member states remain responsible and in which the EU may play a supporting or coordinating role

- protection and improvement of human health
- industry
- culture
- tourism
- education, vocational training, youth and sport
- civil protection
- administrative cooperation

The single market

The single market is one of the European Union's greatest achievements. Restrictions on trade and free competition between member countries have gradually been eliminated, thus helping standards of living to rise.

The single market has not yet become a single economy: some sectors (in particular services of general interest) are still subject to national laws. Freedom to provide services is beneficial, as it stimulates economic activity.

The financial crisis in 2008-09 has led the EU to tighten up its financial legislation.

Over the years the EU has introduced a number of policies (on transport, competition, etc.) to help ensure that as many businesses and consumers as possible benefit from opening up the single market.

I. ACHIEVING THE 1993 OBJECTIVE

(a) The limits of the common market
The 1957 Treaty establishing the European Economic Community (EEC) made it possible to abolish customs barriers between the member countries and to apply a common customs tariff to goods from non-EEC countries. This objective was achieved on 1 July 1968.

However, customs duties are only one aspect of protectionism. In the 1970s, other trade barriers hampered the complete achievement of the common market. Technical norms, health and safety standards, exchange controls and national regulations on the right to practise certain professions all restricted the free movement of people, goods and capital.

(b) The 1993 objective
In June 1985, the Commission, under its President Jacques Delors, published a White Paper setting out plans to abolish, within seven years, all physical, technical and tax-related barriers to free movement within the EEC. The aim was to stimulate the growth of trade and industrial activity within the 'single market' – a large, unified economic area on a par with the United States.

Negotiations between the member state governments led to a new treaty – the Single European Act, which came into force in July 1987. Its provisions included:

▸ extending the powers of the EEC in some policy areas (such as social policy, research and the environment);

▸ establishing the single market by the end of 1992;

▸ making more frequent use of majority voting in the Council of Ministers, to make it easier to take decisions about the single market.

II. PROGRESS ON BUILDING THE SINGLE MARKET

(a) Physical barriers
All border controls within the EU on goods have been abolished, together with customs controls on people, but the police still carry out random spot checks as part of the fight against crime and drugs.

In June 1985, five of the 10 member states signed the Schengen Agreement under which their national police forces undertook to work together, and a common asylum and visa policy was set up. This made it possible to completely abolish checks on persons at the borders between the Schengen countries (see Chapter 10: 'A Europe of freedom, security and justice). Today, the Schengen area is made up of 25 European countries, including three (Iceland, Norway and Switzerland) which are not members of the European Union.

(b) Technical barriers

EU countries have agreed to recognise one another's rules on the sale of most goods. Since the famous 'Cassis de Dijon' ruling by the European Court of Justice in 1979, any product legally manufactured and sold in one member state must be allowed to be placed on the market in all others.

Where services are concerned, EU countries mutually recognise or coordinate their national rules allowing people to practise professions such as law, medicine, tourism, banking or insurance. However, freedom of movement for persons is far from complete. In spite of the 2005 directive on the recognition of professional qualifications, obstacles still hinder people from moving to another EU country or doing certain types of work there. Nevertheless, qualified people (whether lawyers or doctors, builders or plumbers) are increasingly free to practise their profession anywhere in the European Union.

The European Commission has taken action to improve worker mobility, and particularly to ensure that educational diplomas and job qualifications obtained in one EU country are recognised in all the others.

(c) Tax barriers

Tax barriers have been reduced by partially aligning national VAT rates, which must be agreed by the EU member states. Moreover, in July 2005, an agreement came into force between the EU member states and some other countries (including Switzerland) on taxing investment income.

(d) Public contracts

Regardless of who awards them, public contracts in any EU country are now open to bidders from anywhere in the EU. This is thanks to EU directives covering services, supplies and works in many sectors, including water, energy and telecommunications.

© Rolf Bruderer/Corbis

By opening up the telecommunications market to competition, the EU has brought about drastic cost reductions.

The single market benefits all consumers. For example, opening up national markets for services has brought down the price of national telephone calls to a fraction of what they were 10 years ago. Helped by new technology, the Internet is being increasingly used for telephone calls. Competitive pressure has also significantly reduced air fares in Europe.

III. WORK IN PROGRESS

(a) Financial services
In 2008, in the wake of the 'sub-prime' mortgage crisis in the United States, a massive financial crisis rocked the world's banking systems and economies, and plunged the European Union into recession in 2009. At the EU's initiative, the G-20 met in London on 2 April 2009. Its members committed themselves to reforming the financial system so as to make it more transparent and accountable. Europe-wide supervisory authorities will be given responsibility for overseeing hedge funds, providing greater protection for bank deposits, limiting traders' profits and taking more effective steps to prevent and manage crises.

(b) Piracy and counterfeiting
EU products need protection from piracy and counterfeiting. The European Commission estimates that these crimes cost the EU thousands of jobs each year. This is why the Commission and national governments are working on extending copyright and patent protection.

IV. POLICIES UNDERPINNING THE SINGLE MARKET

(a) Transport
The EU's activities have focused mainly on ensuring the freedom to provide services in land transport. In particular, this means giving transport companies free access to the international transport market and allowing transport firms from any EU country to operate in all other EU countries. The EU is also working to ensure fair competition in road transport, by (for example) harmonising the rules on worker qualifications and market access, the freedom to establish a business and provide services, driving times and road safety.

Air transport in Europe used to be dominated by national flag carriers and state-owned airports. The single market has changed all that. All EU airlines may now operate air services on any route within the EU and set fares at any level they choose. Consequently, many new routes have been opened up and prices have fallen dramatically. Passengers, airlines, airports and employees have all benefited.

New EU rules on economic and financial governance have helped to clean up and strengthen the banking sector.

Similarly, passengers are benefiting from increasing competition between railway companies. From 2010, for example, stations on high-speed lines in France and Italy are served by both French and Italian trains.

Shipping — whether carried out by European companies or by vessels flying the flag of non-EU countries — is subject to EU competition rules. These rules are intended to combat unfair pricing practices (flags of convenience) and also to address the serious difficulties facing the shipbuilding industry in Europe.

Since the beginning of the 21st century, the European Union has been funding ambitious new technology projects such as the Galileo satellite navigation system, the European rail traffic management system and SESAR — a programme for modernising air navigation systems. Road traffic safety rules (on things like vehicle maintenance, the transport of dangerous goods and the safety of roads) have been made much tougher. Passengers' rights are also better protected thanks to the Charter of Air Passengers' Rights and recent European legislation on rail passengers' rights. A list of unsafe airlines banned within the EU was first published in 2005.

(b) Competition

The EU's competition policy is essential for ensuring that, within the European single market, competition is not only free but also fair. The European Commission implements this policy and, together with the Court of Justice, ensures that it is respected.

The purpose of this policy is to prevent any business cartel, any aid from public authorities or any unfair monopoly from distorting free competition within the single market.

Any agreement falling under the Treaty rules must be notified to the European Commission by the companies or bodies concerned. The Commission may impose a fine directly on any company which breaks the competition rules or fail to make the required notification – as in the case of Microsoft, which was fined € 900 million in 2008.

If an EU member state illegally grants aid, or fails to notify aid, the Commission may demand that it be repaid. The Commission must also be notified of any merger or takeover that could lead to a company having a dominant position in a particular market.

(c) Protecting consumers and public health

EU legislation in this field aims to give all consumers the same degree of financial and health protection, regardless of where in the European Union they live, travel or do their shopping. The need for EU-wide protection came into sharp focus in the late 1990s with scares over food safety issues such as 'mad cow disease' (BSE). To provide a sound scientific foundation for food safety legislation, the European Food Safety Authority (EFSA) was set up in 2002.

Europe-wide consumer protection is needed in many other fields too, which is why there are numerous EU directives on the safety of cosmetics, toys, fireworks, etc. In 1993 the European Medicines Agency (EMEA) was set up to handle applications for European marketing authorisations for medicinal products. No medicine can be marketed in the EU without such an authorisation.

The European Union also takes action to protect consumers from false and misleading advertising, defective products and abuses in areas such as consumer credit and mail-order or Internet selling.

The euro

[7]

▶ The euro is the single currency shared by 17 of the 27 member states of the European Union. It came into use for non-cash transactions in 1999 and for all payments in 2002, when euro notes and coins were issued.

▶ Each of the new EU member states is expected to adopt the euro once it meets the necessary criteria. In the long run, virtually all EU countries should join the euro area.

▶ The euro gives consumers in Europe considerable advantages. Travellers are spared the cost and inconvenience of changing currencies. Shoppers can directly compare prices in different countries. Prices are stable thanks to the European Central Bank, whose job it is to maintain this stability. Moreover, the euro has become a major reserve currency, alongside the US dollar. During the 2008 financial crisis, having a common currency protected euro-area countries from competitive devaluation and from attack by speculators.

▶ The structural weakness of some member states' economies does expose the euro to speculative attacks. To counter this risk, the EU institutions and the 27 member states decided, on 9 May 2010, to set up a 'financial stabilisation mechanism' worth € 750 billion. The key issue for the future is how to achieve closer coordination and greater economic solidarity between the member states, which need to ensure good governance of their public finances and to reduce their budget deficits.

I. HOW THE EURO WAS CREATED

(a) The European monetary system

In 1971, the United States decided to abolish the fixed link between the dollar and the official price of gold, which had ensured global monetary stability after the Second World War. This put an end to the system of fixed exchange rates. The governors of the EEC countries' central banks decided to limit exchange rate fluctuations between their currencies to no more than 2.25 %, thus creating the 'European monetary system' (EMS), which came into operation in March 1979.

(b) From EMS to EMU

At the European Council in Madrid in June 1989, EU leaders adopted a three-stage plan for economic and monetary union (EMU). This plan became part of the Maastricht Treaty on European Union adopted by the European Council in December 1991.

II. ECONOMIC AND MONETARY UNION

(a) The three stages

The first stage, which began on 1 July 1990, involved:

▶ completely free movement of capital within the EU (abolition of exchange controls);

▶ increasing the Structural Funds so as to step up efforts to remove inequalities between European regions;

▶ economic convergence, through the multilateral surveillance of member states' economic policies.

The second stage began on 1 January 1994. It involved:

▶ setting up the European Monetary Institute (EMI) in Frankfurt; the EMI was made up of the governors of the central banks of the EU countries;

▶ making (or keeping) national central banks independent of government control;

▶ introducing rules to curb national budget deficits.

The third stage was the birth process of the euro. From 1 January 1999 to 1 January 2002, the euro was phased in as the common currency of EU countries that participated (Austria, Belgium, Finland, France, Germany, Greece, Ireland, Italy, Luxembourg, the Netherlands, Portugal and Spain). The European Central Bank (ECB) took over from the EMI and became responsible for monetary policy, which was now defined and implemented in the new currency.

Three countries (Denmark, Sweden and the United Kingdom) decided, for political and technical reasons, not to adopt the euro when it was launched. Slovenia joined the euro area in 2007, followed by Cyprus and Malta in 2008 Slovakia in 2009 and Estonia in 2011.

The euro area thus embraces 17 EU countries, and each of the new member states will join once it has met the necessary conditions.

(b) The convergence criteria

In order to join the euro area, each EU country must meet the following five convergence criteria.

▶ **Price stability:** the rate of inflation may not exceed by more than 1.5 % the average rates of inflation of the three member states with the lowest inflation.

▶ **Interest rates:** long-term interest rates may not vary by more than 2 % in relation to the average interest rates of the three member states with the lowest interest rates.

▶ **Deficits:** national budget deficits must be below 3 % of GDP.

▶ **Public debt:** this may not exceed 60 % of GDP.

▶ **Exchange rate stability:** exchange rates must have remained within the authorised margin of fluctuation for the previous two years.

(c) The Stability and Growth Pact

In June 1997, the Amsterdam European Council adopted a Stability and Growth Pact. This was a permanent commitment to budgetary stability, and made it possible for penalties to be imposed on any country in the euro area whose budget deficit exceeded 3 % of GDP. The Pact was subsequently judged to be too strict and was reformed in March 2005.

(d) The Eurogroup

The Eurogroup consists of the finance ministers from the euro-area countries. They meet to coordinate their economic policies and to monitor their countries' budgetary and financial policies. The Eurogroup also represents the euro's interests in international forums.

Tallin, the capital of Estonia, where the euro replaced the 'kroon' in January 2011.

The Treaty of Lisbon gave the Eurogroup formal status. In January 2010 the Prime Minister of Luxembourg, Jean-Claude Juncker, was re-elected President of the Eurogroup for a period of two and a half years.

(e) Macroeconomic convergence since 2007: the effects of the financial crisis

The 2008 financial crisis considerably increased public debt in most EU countries. Nevertheless, the euro shielded the most vulnerable economies from the risk of devaluation as they endured the crisis and faced attacks by speculators.

Some heavily indebted countries with worsening budget deficits were particularly targeted by attacks during the winter of 2009-10. That is why, acting on a European Commission proposal, the EU member states decided in May 2010, to set up a 'financial stabilisation mechanism' for the euro area. This will provide up to €750 billion in funds from the member states and the IMF. At the same time, the EU's member states and institutions brought into play provisions of the Treaty of Lisbon designed to strengthen the EU's economic governance: prior discussion of national budget plans; monitoring national economies and tightening the rules on competitiveness; reviewing the sanctions to be applied if countries breach the financial rules.

Thus, in response to global financial and economic change, the European Union is having to take tougher action to ensure that member states manage their budgets responsibly and support one another financially. This is the only way to ensure that the euro remains credible as a single currency and that the member states can, together, face the economic challenges of globalisation. Both the Commission and European Parliament stress the importance of coordinating national economic and social policies, since — in the long run — Europe's common currency is not viable without some form of common economic governance.

8

Building on knowledge and innovation

The Europe 2020 strategy aims to:

▶ respond to globalisation and the economic crisis by making the European economy competitive again (telecommunications, services, energy, new green technologies for sustainable development);

▶ ensure:

• smart growth: fostering knowledge, innovation, education and digital society;

• sustainable growth: promoting a more resource efficient, greener and more competitive economy;

• inclusive growth: fostering a high-employment economy delivering social and territorial cohesion.

At the beginning of the 1990s, two great changes began transforming economies and daily life throughout the world, including Europe. One was globalisation, as economies everywhere became increasingly interdependent. The other was the technological revolution, including the Internet and new information and communication technologies. More recently, the world has been rocked by major crises such as the financial crisis of 2007-09 which caused a severe economic downturn and increased unemployment in Europe.

I. THE LISBON PROCESS

(a) Objectives

As long ago as the Lisbon European Council in March 2000, EU leaders decided that the European economy needed thorough modernisation in order to compete with the United States and emerging world players such as Brazil, China and India. The European social model is based on efficiency and solidarity in fields including healthcare and pensions. In order to preserve that model it would have to be revitalised. Europe's competitiveness would have to be based on knowledge and skills, not on low wages. Some industries were relocating to other parts of the world: to take their place, Europe needed to create jobs in high-value sectors such as the e-economy (using high-capacity broadband networks) and new energy-saving technologies. In short, Europe needed a greener and more high-tech economy.

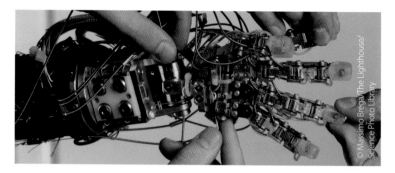

To keep up with global competition, the EU encourages practical use of new technology.

(b) The strategy

The European Council agreed on a detailed strategy for achieving this. The 'Lisbon strategy' involved action in a whole range of areas, such as scientific research, education, vocational training, Internet access and online business. It included reforming Europe's social security systems. These systems are one of Europe's great assets, as they enable our societies to embrace necessary structural and social changes without excessive pain. However, they must be modernised so as to make them sustainable and so that their benefits can be enjoyed by future generations.

Every spring, the European Council meets to review progress in implementing the Lisbon strategy.

II. CLOSER FOCUS ON GROWTH AND JOBS

The European Council in spring 2010 acknowledged that, 10 years on, the Lisbon process had fallen short of its goals. There was still high unemployment in many EU countries and the EU needed to focus on achieving growth and creating jobs. To make its economies more productive and increase social cohesion, Europe must invest more in research and innovation, education and training. So, on the initiative of José Manuel Barroso (President of the European Commission), the European Council adopted a new strategy for the next 10 years: the Europe 2020 strategy.

One of the objectives of 'Europe 2020' is bringing higher education
and the business world closer together.

As part of this strategy, the 27 EU member states will:

▶ give the European Commission a greater role in driving the process forward,
in particular by disseminating 'best practice' in Europe (thus going beyond
the merely inter-governmental approach known as the 'open method of
coordination');

▶ move faster to reform their financial markets and social security systems and
to open up their telecommunications and energy sectors to competition;

▶ improve their education systems, do more to help young people find jobs,
forge stronger links between universities and businesses and continue the
Erasmus, Leonardo and Erasmus Mundus programmes;

▶ take swifter action (e.g. by harmonising their tax and social security
arrangements) to create a European 'single market' for research – enabling
scientists, knowledge and technology to move freely around Europe;

▶ increase spending on research and innovation to 3 % of GDP (a goal also
adopted by the United States).

9

What does it mean to be a European citizen?

▶ Citizens of European Union countries can travel, live and work anywhere in the EU.

▶ The EU encourages and funds programmes, particularly in the fields of education and culture, to bring EU citizens closer together.

▶ A sense of belonging to the European Union will develop only gradually, as the EU achieves tangible results and explains more clearly what it is doing for people.

▶ People recognise symbols of shared European identity such as the single currency and the European flag and anthem.

▶ A 'European public sphere' is beginning to emerge, with Europe-wide political parties. Citizens vote every five years for a new European Parliament, which then votes on the new European Commission.

Citizenship of the European Union is enshrined in the EU Treaty: 'Every person holding the nationality of a member state shall be a citizen of the Union. Citizenship of the Union shall be additional to and not replace national citizenship' (Article 20(1) of the Treaty on the Functioning of the European Union). But what does EU citizenship mean in practice?

I. TRAVELLING, LIVING AND WORKING IN EUROPE

If you are an EU citizen you have the right to travel, work and live anywhere in the European Union.

If you have completed a university course lasting three years or more, your qualification will be recognised in all EU countries, since EU member states have confidence in the quality of one another's education and training systems.

You can work in the health, education and other public services (except for the police, armed forces, etc.) of any country in the European Union. Indeed, what could be more natural than recruiting a British teacher to teach English in Rome, or encouraging a young Belgian graduate to compete in a civil service exam in France?

Before travelling within the EU you can obtain from your national authorities a European health insurance card, to help cover your medical costs if you fall ill while in another country.

© Christophe Vander Eecken/Reporters

Europeans are free to live and work in any EU country that they choose.

II. HOW YOU CAN EXERCISE YOUR RIGHTS AS A EUROPEAN CITIZEN

As a citizen of the European Union you are not just a worker or a consumer: you also have specific political rights. Since the Maastricht Treaty came into force, regardless of your nationality, you have had the right to vote and to stand as a candidate in local elections in your country of residence and in elections to the European Parliament.

As of December 2009 (when the Treaty of Lisbon came into force), you also have the right to petition the Commission to put forward a legislative proposal — provided you can find a million people from a significant number of EU countries to sign your petition.

III. FUNDAMENTAL RIGHTS

The European Union's commitment to citizens' rights was made clear at Nice in December 2000 when the European Council solemnly proclaimed the **Charter of Fundamental Rights of the European Union**. This Charter had been drawn up by a Convention composed of members of national parliaments, MEPs, representatives of national governments and a member of the European Commission. Under six headings — Dignity, Freedoms, Equality, Solidarity, Citizens' rights and Justice — its 54 articles set out the European Union's fundamental values and the civil, political, economic and social rights of EU citizens.

The opening articles cover human dignity, the right to life, the right to the 'integrity of the person' and the right to freedom of expression and of conscience. The chapter on solidarity brings together, in an innovative way, social and economic rights such as:

▶ the right to strike;

▶ the right of workers to be informed and consulted;

▶ the right to reconcile family life and professional life;

▶ the right to healthcare, social security and social assistance throughout the European Union.

The Charter also promotes equality between men and women and introduces rights such as data protection, a ban on eugenic practices and the reproductive cloning of human beings, the right to environmental protection, the rights of children and elderly people and the right to good administration.

The Treaty of Lisbon, which came into force on 1 December 2009, gives the Charter the same legal force as the Treaties — so it can be used as the basis for taking a case to the EU Court of Justice. (However, a protocol specifies the application of the Charter in Poland and the United Kingdom, and this will later also apply to the Czech Republic).

Moreover, Article 6 of the Treaty of Lisbon provides a legal basis for the EU to sign up to the European Convention on Human Rights. This Convention would then no longer be merely referred to in the EU Treaties but would have legal force in EU countries, thus giving greater protection to human rights in the European Union.

One of the basic rights laid down in the Charter of Fundamental Rights of the European Union is that of balancing family life with a career.

IV. EUROPE MEANS EDUCATION AND CULTURE

A sense of belonging together and having a common destiny cannot be manufactured. It can only arise from a shared cultural awareness, which is why Europe needs to focus not just on economics but also on education, citizenship and culture.

The EU does not say how schools and education are to be organised or what the curriculum is: these things are decided at national or local level. But the EU does run programmes to promote educational exchanges so that young people can go abroad to train or study, learn new languages and take part in joint activities with schools or colleges in other countries. These programmes include Comenius (school education), Erasmus (higher education), Leonardo da Vinci (vocational training), Grundtvig (adult education) and Jean Monnet (university-level teaching and research in European integration).

European countries are working together — via the 'Bologna process' — to create a European higher education area. This means, for example, that university courses in all the countries concerned will lead to comparable and mutually recognised degrees (Bachelor's, Master's and Doctorate).

In the field of culture, the EU's 'Culture' and 'Media' programmes foster cooperation between TV programme and film-makers, promoters, broadcasters and cultural bodies from different countries. This encourages the production of more European TV programmes and films, thereby helping redress the balance between European and American output.

One of Europe's essential characteristics is its diversity of languages — and preserving that diversity is an important EU objective. Indeed, multilingualism is fundamental to the way the European Union works. EU legislation has to be available in all 23 official languages, and every MEP has the right to use his or her own language in parliamentary debates.

V. THE OMBUDSMAN AND YOUR RIGHT TO PETITION PARLIAMENT

To help bring the EU closer to its citizens, the Treaty on European Union created the post of Ombudsman. The European Parliament appoints the Ombudsman, who remains in office for the duration of the Parliament. The Ombudsman's role is to investigate complaints against EU institutions and bodies. Complaints may be brought by any EU citizen and by any person or organisation living or based in an EU country. The Ombudsman tries to arrange an amicable settlement between the complainant and the institution or body concerned.

Anyone living in an EU country can also petition the European Parliament. This is another important link between the EU institutions and the public.

VI. A SENSE OF BELONGING

The idea of a 'citizens' Europe' is very new. Some symbols of a shared European identity already exist, such as the European passport, in use since 1985. EU driving licences have been issued in all EU countries since 1996. The EU has a motto, 'United in diversity', and 9 May is celebrated as 'Europe Day'.

The European anthem (Beethoven's 'Ode to Joy') and the European flag (a circle of 12 gold stars on a blue background) were explicitly mentioned in the 2004 draft Constitution for the European Union, but were dropped from the Lisbon Treaty which replaced it. These are still EU symbols and member states, local authorities and individual citizens may use them if they wish.

However, people cannot feel they 'belong to' the European Union unless they are aware of what the EU is doing and understand why. The EU institutions and member states need to do much more to explain EU affairs in clear and simple language.

People also need to see the EU making a tangible difference to their daily lives. In this respect, the use of euro notes and coins since 2002 has had a major impact. More than two thirds of EU citizens now manage their personal budget and savings in euro. Pricing goods and services in euro means that consumers can compare prices directly from one country to another.

Border checks have been abolished between most EU countries under the Schengen Agreement, and this already gives people a sense of belonging to a single, unified geographical area.

A sense of belonging comes, above all, with feeling personally involved in EU decision-making. Every adult EU citizen has the right to vote in European Parliament elections, and this is an important basis for the EU's democratic legitimacy. That legitimacy is being increased as more powers are given to the European Parliament, national parliaments have a greater say in EU business and Europe's citizens become more actively involved in NGOs, in political movements and in setting up Europe-wide political parties. If you want to help shape the European agenda and influence EU policies, there are many ways to do so. There are, for example, online discussion forums dedicated to European Union affairs where you can join in the debate, and you can post your views on Commissioners' or MEPs' blogs. You can also contact the Commission or Parliament directly, online or via one of their offices in your country (see the inside back cover for details).

The European Union was set up to serve the peoples of Europe, and its future must be shaped by the active involvement of people from all walks of life. The EU's founding fathers were well aware of this. 'We are not bringing together states, we are uniting people', said Jean Monnet back in 1952. Raising public awareness about the EU and involving citizens in its activities is still one of the greatest challenges facing the EU institutions today.

10

A Europe of freedom, security and justice

▸ The opening of internal borders between EU member states is a very tangible benefit for ordinary people, allowing them to travel freely without being subject to border controls.

▸ However, this freedom of internal movement must go hand in hand with increased controls at the EU's external borders so as to effectively combat organised crime, terrorism, illegal immigration and the trafficking of people and drugs.

▸ The EU countries cooperate in the area of policing and justice so as to make Europe safer and more secure.

European citizens are entitled to live in freedom, without fear of persecution or violence, anywhere in the European Union. Yet international crime and terrorism are among the main concerns of Europeans today.

Clearly, freedom of movement must mean giving everyone, everywhere in the EU, the same protection and the same access to justice. So, through successive amendments to the Treaties, the European Union is gradually being made into a single 'area of freedom, security and justice'.

The scope for EU action in these fields has been widened, over the years, as the European Council adopted three successive framework programmes: the Tampere programme (1999-2004), the Hague programme (2005-09) and the Stockholm programme (2010-14). While the Tampere and Hague programmes aimed at greater security, Stockholm focuses more on protecting citizens' rights.

Decision-making in these fields has become more effective thanks to the Lisbon Treaty, which came into force in December 2009. Until then, the member states had reserved for themselves all responsibility for creating and managing the area of freedom, security and justice. The work was carried out essentially by the Council (i.e. through discussion and agreement between government ministers), leaving the Commission and Parliament to play only a small role. The Lisbon Treaty has changed that: the Council now takes most of its decisions by a qualified majority vote and Parliament is an equal partner in the decision-making process.

I. MOVING FREELY WITHIN THE EU AND PROTECTING ITS EXTERNAL BORDERS

The free movement of people within the EU raises security issues for the member states, since they no longer control internal EU borders. To compensate for this, extra security measures have to be put in place at the EU's external borders. Moreover, since criminals can also exploit freedom of movement within the EU, national police forces and judicial authorities have to work together to combat cross-border crime.

One of the most important moves to make life easier for travellers in the European Union took place in 1985, when the governments of Belgium, France, the Federal Republic of Germany, Luxembourg and the Netherlands signed an agreement in a small Luxembourg border town called Schengen. They agreed to abolish all checks on people, regardless of nationality, at their shared borders, to harmonise controls at their borders with non-EU countries and to introduce a common policy on visas. They thus formed an area without internal frontiers known as the Schengen area.

The Schengen arrangements have since become an integral part of the EU Treaties, and the Schengen area has gradually expanded. In 2010, the Schengen rules are fully implemented by all EU countries except Bulgaria, Cyprus, Ireland, Romania and the United Kingdom. Three non-EU countries — Iceland, Norway and Switzerland — are also in the Schengen area.

Tightening up checks at the EU's external borders became a priority when the EU expanded in 2004 and 2007. An EU agency known as Frontex, based in Warsaw, is responsible for managing EU cooperation on external border security. The member states can lend it boats, helicopters and planes for carrying out joint patrols — for example in sensitive areas of the Mediterranean. The EU is also considering setting up a European border guard service.

As the EU's population ages, legal immigrants with the right qualifications are helping to bridge the gaps in the labour market.

II. ASYLUM AND IMMIGRATION POLICY

Europe is proud of its humanitarian tradition of welcoming foreigners and offering asylum to refugees fleeing danger and persecution. Today, however, EU governments face the pressing question of how to deal with rising numbers of immigrants, both legal and illegal, in an area without internal frontiers.

EU governments have agreed to harmonise their rules so that, by 2012, applications for asylum can be processed in accordance with a set of basic principles uniformly recognised throughout the European Union. Some technical measures have been adopted, such as minimum standards for admitting asylum-seekers and for granting refugee status.

In recent years, large numbers of illegal immigrants have been arriving on Europe's shores, and one of the EU's top priorities is to deal with this problem. Member governments are working together to tackle people smuggling and to agree common arrangements for repatriating illegal immigrants. At the same time, legal immigration is being better coordinated under EU rules on family reunification, on the status of long-term residents and on admitting non-EU nationals who wish to come to Europe to study or to undertake research.

Cooperation between European customs authorities is helping to reduce trafficking and crime.

III. FIGHTING INTERNATIONAL CRIME

A coordinated effort is needed to combat criminal gangs who run people-trafficking networks and who exploit vulnerable human beings, particularly women and children.

Organised crime is becoming ever more sophisticated and regularly uses European or international networks for its activities. Terrorism has clearly shown that it can strike, with great brutality, anywhere in the world.

This is why the Schengen information system (SIS) was set up. This is a complex database which enables police forces and judicial authorities to exchange information on people for whom an arrest warrant or extradition request has been issued, and on stolen property such as vehicles or works of art. A new generation database known as SIS II will have a greater capacity and make it possible to store new types of data.

One of the best ways of catching criminals is to track their ill-gotten gains. For this reason, and to cut off the funding of criminal and terrorist organisations, the EU has brought in legislation to prevent money-laundering.

The greatest advance made in recent years in the field of cooperation between law enforcement authorities was the creation of Europol, an EU body based in The Hague and staffed by police and customs officers. It tackles a wide range of international crime: drug trafficking, trade in stolen vehicles, people trafficking and illegal immigration networks, the sexual exploitation of women and children, child pornography, forgery, the trafficking of radioactive and nuclear material, terrorism, money-laundering and counterfeiting the euro.

IV. TOWARDS A 'EUROPEAN JUDICIAL AREA'

At present, many different judicial systems operate side by side in the European Union, each within national borders. But international crime and terrorism have no respect for national boundaries. This is why the EU needs a common framework for fighting terrorism, drug trafficking and counterfeiting, so as to guarantee its citizens a high level of protection and to improve international cooperation in this area. The EU also needs a common criminal justice policy, to ensure that cooperation between the courts in different countries is not hampered by their differing definitions of certain criminal acts.

The main example of practical cooperation in this field is Eurojust, a central coordinating structure established in The Hague in 2003. Its purpose is to enable the national investigating and prosecuting authorities to work together on criminal investigations involving several EU countries. On the basis of Eurojust, a European Public Prosecutor's Office may be set up — if the Council (or a group of at least nine member states) so decides. The role of the prosecutor would be to investigate and prosecute offences against the EU's financial interests.

Another tool for practical cross-border cooperation is the European arrest warrant, operational since January 2004. It is intended to replace lengthy extradition procedures.

In the area of civil law, the EU has adopted legislation to help apply court rulings in cross-border cases involving divorce, separation, child custody and maintenance claims. The aim is to ensure that judgments in one country are applicable in another. The EU has established common procedures to simplify and speed up the settlement of cross-border cases in small and uncontested civil claims like debt recovery and bankruptcy.

[11]

▶ The European Union has more influence on the world stage when it speaks with a single voice in international affairs such as trade negotiations. To help achieve this, and to raise the EU's international profile, in 2009 the European Council acquired a permanent President and the first High Representative of the Union for Foreign Affairs and Security Policy was appointed.

▶ In the area of defence, each country remains sovereign, whether a member of NATO or neutral. However, the EU member states are developing military cooperation for peacekeeping missions.

▶ The EU is a major player in international trade, and is working within the World Trade Organisation (WTO) to ensure open markets and a rules-based trading system.

▶ For historical and geographical reasons, the EU pays particularly close attention to Africa (via development aid policies, trade preferences, food aid and promoting respect for human rights).

In economic, trade and monetary terms, the European Union has become a major world power. It is sometimes said that the EU has become an economic giant but remained a political dwarf. This is an exaggeration. The European Union has considerable influence within international organisations such as the World Trade Organisation (WTO) and the specialised bodies of the United Nations (UN), and at world summits on the environment and development.

Nevertheless, it is true that the EU and its members have a long way to go, in diplomatic and political terms, before they can speak with one voice on major world issues. What is more, military defence (the cornerstone of national sovereignty) remains in the hands of national governments, whose ties are those forged within alliances such as NATO.

I. THE COMMON FOREIGN AND SECURITY POLICY

(a) Setting up a European diplomatic service

The common foreign and security policy (CFSP) and the European security and defence policy (ESDP), define the EU's main foreign policy tasks. These policies were introduced by the Treaties of Maastricht (1992), Amsterdam (1997) and Nice (2001). They formed the EU's 'second pillar' – a policy area in which action is decided by intergovernmental agreement and in which the Commission and the Parliament play only a minor role. Decisions in this area are taken by consensus, although individual states can abstain. Although the Treaty of Lisbon did away with 'pillars' in the EU's structure, it did not change the way in which security and defence matters are decided. However, it changed the policy's name from ESDP to CSDP – the common security and defence policy. It also raised the profile of the CFSP by creating the post of High Representative of the Union for Foreign Affairs and Security Policy.

Since 1 December 2009, this post has been occupied by Catherine Ashton, from the United Kingdom, who is also a Vice-President of the European Commission. Her job is to represent the EU's collective viewpoint and to act in the EU's name within international organisations and at international conferences. She is assisted by the thousands of EU and national officials who make up the European External Action Service – in effect, the EU's diplomatic service.

The aim of EU foreign policy is, essentially, to ensure security, stability, democracy and respect for human rights — not only in its immediate neighbourhood (e.g. the Balkans) but also in other hot spots around the world, such as in Africa, the Middle East and the Caucasus. Its main tool is 'soft power', which covers things like election observation missions, humanitarian aid and development assistance. In 2009, the EU donated humanitarian aid worth € 900 million to 30 countries, mostly in Africa. The EU provides 60 % of the world's development assistance and helps the world's most needy countries to fight poverty, feed their people, avoid natural disasters, access drinking water and fight disease. At the same time, the EU actively encourages these countries to respect the rule of law and to open up their markets to international trade. The Commission and the European Parliament are careful to ensure that the aid is provided in an accountable manner and is properly managed and used.

Is the EU able and willing to go further than this 'soft power' diplomacy? That is the main challenge for the years ahead. All too often, the European Council's joint statements and common positions on major international issues (the Middle East peace process, Iraq, terrorism, relations with Russia, Iran, Cuba, etc.) express nothing but the lowest common denominator. Meanwhile, the large member states continue to play their own individual diplomatic roles. Yet it is when the European Union speaks with one voice that it is seen as a global player. If its credibility and influence are to grow, the EU must combine its economic might and trading power with the steady implementation of its common security and defence policy.

(b) Tangible achievements of the common security and defence policy (CSDP)

Since 2003, the European Union has had the capacity to carry out crisis management operations, as the member states voluntarily make some of their own forces available to the EU for performing such operations.

Responsibility for running the operations lies with a set of politico-military bodies: the Political and Security Committee (PSC), the EU Military Committee (EUMC), the Committee for Civilian Aspects of Crisis Management (Civcom) and the European Union Military Staff (EUMS). These bodies are answerable to the Council and are based in Brussels.

This set of tools is what gives substance to the common security and defence policy. It enables the EU to carry out the tasks it has set itself — humanitarian and peacemaking or peacekeeping missions. These missions must avoid duplicating what NATO is doing, and this is guaranteed by the 'Berlin plus' arrangements agreed between NATO and the EU. They give the European Union access to NATO's logistical resources (for detection, communication, command and transport).

Since 2003, the European Union has launched 22 military operations and civilian missions. The first of these was in Bosnia and Herzegovina, where EU troops replaced NATO forces. These missions and operations, under the European flag, are being or have been deployed on three continents. They include the EUFOR mission in Chad and the Central African Republic, Eunavfor's 'Atalanta' operation to combat Somali piracy in the Gulf of Aden, the EULEX mission to help Kosovo firmly establish the rule of law, and the EUPOL mission in Afghanistan to help train the Afghan police.

The EU runs civil or military peacekeeping operations such as this anti-piracy force off the coast of Somalia.

As military technology becomes ever more sophisticated and expensive, EU governments are finding it increasingly necessary to work together on arms manufacture – especially now that they are striving to reduce public spending to help them weather the financial crisis. Moreover, if their armed forces are to carry out joint missions outside Europe, their systems must be interoperable and their equipment sufficiently standardised. This is why the Thessaloniki European Council in June 2003 decided to set up a European Defence Agency (EDA) to help develop the EU's military capabilities. It was formally established in 2004.

II. A TRADE POLICY THAT IS OPEN TO THE WORLD

Its importance as a trading power gives the European Union considerable international influence. The EU supports the rules-based system of the World Trade Organisation (WTO), which has 153 member countries. This system provides a degree of legal certainty and transparency in the conduct of international trade. The WTO sets conditions under which its members can defend themselves against unfair practices like dumping (selling below cost) through which exporters compete against their rivals. It also provides a procedure for settling disputes that arise between two or more trading partners.

Since 2001, through the 'Doha round' of trade talks, the EU has been seeking to open up world trade. These are difficult negotiations but the EU remains convinced that, in the wake of the financial and economic crisis, a contraction in world trade would turn the recession into a full-blown depression.

The EU's trade policy is closely linked to its development policy. Under its 'general system of preferences' (GSP), the EU has granted duty-free or cut-rate preferential access to its market for most of the imports from developing countries and economies in transition. It goes even further for the world's 49 poorest countries. All of their exports, with the sole exception of arms, enjoy duty-free entry to the EU market.

The EU does not, however, have specific trade agreements with its major trading partners among the developed countries like the United States and Japan. Here, trade relations are handled through the WTO mechanisms. The United States and the European Union are seeking to develop relations founded on equality and partnership. Following the election of Barack Obama as US President, EU leaders have been calling for closer trans-Atlantic ties. At the G-20 meeting in London in April 2009, the EU and US agreed on the need for better regulation of the global financial system.

The EU promotes the opening of markets and the development of trade within the multilateral framework of the World Trade Organisation.

The European Union is increasing its trade with the emerging powers in other parts of the world, from China and India to Central and South America. Trade agreements with these countries also involve technical and cultural cooperation. China has become the EU's second most important trading partner (after the United States) and its biggest supplier of imports. (In 2009, more than 17 % of the EU's imports came from China). The European Union is Russia's main trading partner and its biggest source of foreign investment. Apart from trade, the main issues in EU-Russia relations concern cross-border matters such as the security of energy supplies, in particular gas.

III. AFRICA

Relations between Europe and sub-Saharan Africa go back a long way. Under the Treaty of Rome in 1957, the then colonies and overseas territories of member states became associates of the Community. Decolonisation, which began in the early 1960s, turned this link into a different kind of association, one between sovereign countries.

The Cotonou Agreement, signed in 2000 in Cotonou, the capital of Benin, marked a new stage in the EU's development policy. This agreement between the European Union and the African, Caribbean and Pacific (ACP) countries is the most ambitious and far-reaching trade and aid agreement ever concluded between developed and developing countries. It followed on from the Lomé Convention, which was signed in 1975 in Lomé, the capital of Togo, and subsequently updated at regular intervals.

This agreement goes significantly further than earlier ones, since it has moved from trade relations based on market access to trade relations in a wider sense. It also introduces new procedures for dealing with human rights abuses.

The European Union has granted special trading concessions to the least developed countries, 39 of which are signatories to the Cotonou Agreement. Since 2005, they have been able to export practically any type of product to the EU, duty free. In 2009, the EU agreed to provide the 77 ACP countries with € 2.7 billion of aid in the fields of health, water, climate change and peacekeeping.

What future for Europe?

▶ 'Europe will not be made all at once, or according
to a single plan. It will be built through concrete
achievements which first create a de facto solidarity.'

▶ This statement from 1950 is still true. But what are the
great challenges for Europe in the coming years?

'Europe will not be made all at once, or according to a single plan. It will be built through concrete achievements which first create a de facto solidarity'. So said Robert Schuman in his famous Declaration, launching the European integration project on 9 May 1950. Sixty years on, his words are as true as ever. The solidarity between Europe's peoples and nations must constantly be adapted to deal with new challenges posed by a changing world. Completion of the single market in the early 1990s was a great achievement, but it was not enough. To make the market work effectively, the euro had to be invented — making its appearance in 1999. To manage the euro and ensure price stability, the European Central Bank was set up: but the financial crisis of 2008-09 and the debt crisis of 2010 showed that the euro is vulnerable to attack by global speculators. What is needed, in addition to the ECB, is coordination of national economic policies — a much closer coordination than currently provided by the Eurogroup. So, will the EU soon be laying plans for genuinely shared economic governance?

Jean Monnet, the great architect of European integration, concluded his 1976 memoirs with these words: 'The sovereign nations of the past can no longer solve the problems of the present: they cannot ensure their own progress or control their own future. And the Community itself is only a stage on the way to the organised world of tomorrow'. Given today's global economy, should we already regard the European Union as no longer politically relevant? Or should we rather be asking how to unleash the full potential of half a billion Europeans who share the same values and interests?

The European Union will soon have more than 30 member states, with very different histories, languages and cultures. Can such a diverse family of nations form a common political 'public sphere'? Can its citizens develop a shared sense of 'being European' while remaining deeply attached to their country, their region and their local community? Perhaps they can, if today's member states follow the example of the very first European Community — the ECSC — which was born from the rubble of the Second World War. Its moral legitimacy was based on reconciliation and consolidating the peace between former enemies. It adhered to the principle that all member states, whether large or small, had equal rights and respected minorities.

Will it be possible to keep pushing ahead with European integration, claiming that the EU's member states and their peoples all want the same thing? Or will EU leaders make greater use of 'reinforced cooperation' arrangements, whereby ad hoc groups of member states can move ahead without the others in this or that direction? The multiplication of such arrangements could lead to an à la carte or 'variable geometry' Europe, with each member state free to choose whether to pursue a particular policy or to be part of a particular institution. This solution might appear attractively simple, but it would be the beginning of the end for the EU, which works by anticipating the common interests of its member states, in both the short and the long term. It is based on the concept of solidarity — which means sharing the costs as well as the advantages. It means having common rules and common policies. Exemptions, derogations and opt-outs should be exceptional and of short duration. Transitional arrangements and phasing-in periods may sometimes be necessary, but unless all the member states keep to the same rules and work towards the same goals, solidarity breaks down and the advantages of being in a strong and united Europe are lost.

Globalisation obliges Europe to compete not only with its traditional rivals (Japan and the US) but also with fast-rising economic powers such as Brazil, China and India. Can it continue restricting access to its single market in order to protect its social and environmental standards? Even if it did so, there would be no escape from the harsh realities of international competition. The only solution is for Europe to become a real global player, acting in unison on the world stage and asserting its interests effectively by speaking with one voice. Progress in this direction can only be achieved by moving towards political union. The President of the European Council, the Commission President and the High Representative of the Union for Foreign Affairs and Security Policy must together give the EU strong and consistent leadership.

At the same time, the EU needs to become more democratic. The European Parliament — which has been given greater power with each new treaty — is directly elected by universal suffrage every five years. But the percentage of the population actually voting in these elections varies from country to country, and the turnout is often low. The challenge for the EU's institutions and national governments is to find better ways of informing and communicating with the public (through education, NGO networks, etc.) and thus foster the emergence of a common European public sphere in which EU citizens can shape the political agenda.

Europeans need to work together today for their future tomorrow.

Finally, Europe should punch its full weight in international affairs. One of the EU's great strengths is its ability to spread European values beyond its borders. Values such as respecting human rights, upholding the rule of law, protecting the environment and maintaining social standards in the social market economy. Imperfect as it is, the EU can hardly claim to be a shining model for the rest of humanity. But to the extent that Europe is successful, other regions will look to it as an example. What would count as success for the EU in the years ahead? Bringing its public finances back into balance. Coping with the ageing of its population in a way that does not unfairly penalise the next generation. Finding ethical responses to the huge challenges posed by scientific and technological progress — particularly in biotechnology. Ensuring security for its citizens without undermining their freedom. If it can do these things, Europe will continue to be respected and will remain a source of inspiration to the rest of the world.

Key dates
in the history of
European integration

1950	**9 May** – Robert Schuman, the French Minister for Foreign Affairs, makes an important speech putting forward proposals based on the ideas of Jean Monnet. He proposes that France and the Federal Republic of Germany pool their coal and steel resources in a new organisation which other European countries can join.
1951	**18 April** – In Paris, six countries – Belgium, the Federal Republic of Germany, France, Italy, Luxembourg and the Netherlands – sign the Treaty establishing the European Coal and Steel Community (ECSC). It comes into force on 23 July 1952, for a period of 50 years.
1955	**1-2 June** – At a meeting in Messina, the foreign ministers of the six countries decide to extend European integration to the economy as a whole.
1957	**25 March** – In Rome, the six countries sign the Treaties establishing the European Economic Community (EEC) and the European Atomic Energy Community (Euratom). They come into force on 1 January 1958.
1960	**4 January** – At the instigation of the United Kingdom, the Stockholm Convention establishes the European Free Trade Association (EFTA), comprising a number of European countries that are not part of the EEC.
1963	**20 July** – In Yaoundé, an association agreement is signed between the EEC and 18 African countries.
1965	**8 April** – A treaty is signed merging the executive bodies of the three Communities (the ECSC, EEC and Euratom) and creating a single Council and a single Commission. It comes into force on 1 July 1967.
1966	**29 January** – The 'Luxembourg compromise': following a political crisis, France agrees to take part in Council meetings once again, in return for an agreement that the unanimity rule be maintained when 'vital national interests' are at stake.
1968	**1 July** – Customs duties between the member states on industrial goods are completely abolished, 18 months ahead of schedule, and a common external tariff is introduced.
1969	**1-2 December** – At the Hague Summit, the EEC's political leaders decide to move further ahead with European integration.
1970	**22 April** – In Luxembourg, a treaty is signed allowing the European Communities to be increasingly financed from 'own resources' and giving greater supervisory powers to the European Parliament.
1973	**1 January** – Denmark, Ireland and the United Kingdom join the European Communities, bringing their membership to nine. Norway stays out, following a referendum.

1974	**9-10 December** – At the Paris Summit, the political leaders of the nine member states decide to meet three times a year as the European Council. They also give the go-ahead for direct elections to the European Parliament, and agree to set up the European Regional Development Fund.
1975	**28 February** – In Lomé, a convention (Lomé I) is signed between the EEC and 46 African, Caribbean and Pacific (ACP) countries. **22 July** – A treaty is signed giving the European Parliament greater power over the budget and establishing the European Court of Auditors. It comes into force on 1 June 1977.
1979	**7-10 June** – The first direct elections to the 410-seat European Parliament.
1981	**1 January** – Greece joins the European Communities, bringing the number of members to 10.
1984	**14 and 17 June** – The second direct elections to the European Parliament.
1985	**7 January** – Jacques Delors becomes President of the Commission (1985-95). **14 June** – The Schengen Agreement is signed with the aim of abolishing checks at the borders between member countries of the European Communities.
1986	**1 January** – Spain and Portugal join the European Communities, bringing their membership to 12. **17 and 28 February** – The Single European Act is signed in Luxembourg and The Hague. It comes into force on 1 July 1987.
1989	**15 and 18 June** – The third direct elections to the European Parliament. **9 November** – The fall of the Berlin Wall.
1990	**3 octobre** – German unification.
1991	**9-10 December** – The Maastricht European Council adopts a Treaty on European Union. This lays the foundation for a common foreign and security policy, closer cooperation on justice and home affairs and the creation of economic and monetary union, including a single currency.
1992	**7 February** – The Treaty on European Union is signed at Maastricht. It comes into force on 1 November 1993.
1993	**1 January** – The single market is created.
1994	**9 and 12 June** – The fourth direct elections to the European Parliament.

1995	**1 January** – Austria, Finland and Sweden join the EU, bringing its membership to 15. Norway stays out, again following a referendum.
	23 January – A new European Commission takes office with Jacques Santer as its President (1995-99).
	27-28 November – The Euro-Mediterranean Conference in Barcelona launches a partnership between the EU and the countries on the southern shore of the Mediterranean.
1997	**2 October** – The Amsterdam Treaty is signed. It comes into force on 1 May 1999.
1998	**30 March** – The accession process begins for the new candidate countries – Cyprus, Malta and 10 central and eastern European countries.
1999	**1 January** – Eleven EU countries adopt the euro, which is launched on the financial markets, replacing their currencies for non-cash transactions. The European Central Bank takes on responsibility for monetary policy. On 1 January 2001, Greece becomes the 12th country to adopt the euro.
	10 and 13 June – The fifth direct elections to the European Parliament.
	15 September – A new European Commission takes office with Romano Prodi as its President (1999-2004).
	15-16 October – The Tampere European Council decides to make the EU an area of freedom, security and justice.
2000	**23-24 March** – The Lisbon European Council draws up a new strategy for boosting employment in the EU, modernising the economy and strengthening social cohesion in a knowledge-based Europe.
	7-8 December – In Nice, the European Council reaches agreement on the text of a new treaty changing the EU's decision-making system so that the Union will be ready for enlargement. The Presidents of the European Parliament, the European Council and the European Commission solemnly proclaim the Charter of Fundamental Rights of the European Union.
2001	**26 February** – The Treaty of Nice is signed. It comes into force on 1 February 2003.
	14-15 December – Laeken European Council: a declaration on the future of the EU is agreed. This opens the way for the forthcoming major reform of the EU and for the creation of a Convention (chaired by Valéry Giscard d'Estaing) to draft a European Constitution.
2002	**1 January** – Euro notes and coins are introduced in the 12 euro-area countries.
2003	**10 July** – The Convention on the Future of Europe completes its work on the draft European Constitution.

| 2004 | **1 May** – Cyprus, the Czech Republic, Estonia, Hungary, Latvia, Lithuania, Malta, Poland, Slovakia and Slovenia join the European Union. |

10 and 13 June – The sixth direct elections to the European Parliament.

29 October – The European Constitution is signed in Rome by the 25 Heads of State or Government.

22 November – A new European Commission takes office with José Manuel Barroso as its President.

2005   **29 May and 1 June** – Voters in France reject the Constitution in a referendum, followed three days later by voters in the Netherlands.

3 October – Accession negotiations begin with Turkey and Croatia.

2007   **1 January** – Bulgaria and Romania join the European Union. Slovenia becomes the 13th country to adopt the euro.

13 December – The Treaty of Lisbon is signed.

2008   **1 January** – Cyprus and Malta become the 14th and the 15th countries to adopt the euro.

2009   **1 January** – Slovakia becomes the 16th country to adopt the euro.

4-7 June – The seventh direct elections to the European Parliament.

2 October – A referendum in Ireland approves the Treaty of Lisbon.

1 December – The Treaty of Lisbon comes into force. Herman Van Rompuy becomes President of the European Council and Catherine Ashton becomes High Representative of the Union for Foreign Affairs and Security Policy.

2010   **9 February** – The European Parliament gives its consent to the new European Commission, with José Manuel Barroso as its President for the second time.

9 May – A European Financial Stabilisation Mechanism is created, worth € 750 billion.

2011   **1 January** – Estonia becomes the 17th country to adopt the euro.

NOTES

The European Union

	Member States of the European Union
	Candidate countries